THE OFFICIAL
ANNUAL 2011

A Grange Publication

Written by Michael Bridge
Designed by Colin Heggie

© 2010. Published by Grange Communications Ltd., Edinburgh, under licence from Tottenham Hotspur PLC.
Printed in the EU.

Photography © Action Images

ISBN: 978-1-907104-76-3

£7.99

Contents 2011

Welcome

Dear Supporters

Welcome to the 2011 Official Tottenham Hotspur Annual.

My second season at the club couldn't have gone any better. Finishing fourth was a superb achievement from the players and when you consider the injuries we have had to put up with during the season it really was fantastic.

At the start of last season the coaching staff and I were aiming for a top six finish if all our key player stayed fit. But we continued to pick up points and in the end we fully deserved our shot at Champions League football. It certainly is a squad game and every player that came into the side stepped up and did the job. I knew when I joined Spurs we didn't have to radically change the squad, just tweak it in certain areas.

Looking back on the season in depth, victories over Arsenal, Chelsea, Liverpool and of course, our win at Manchester City will live long in the memory. Then there is the amazing 9-1 victory over Wigan to think about. That was a great day and one which will not be repeated in a long time I'm sure.

We couldn't have achieved any of our success if it wasn't for our fantastic supporters. Don't underestimate just how much we appreciate your wonderful backing home and away. We're now looking to build on our fourth place finish but it won't be easy. Teams will improve and we must be ready as our league is getting stronger each year. I look forward to seeing you at the Lane for what I'm sure will be another exciting season.

All the best,

Harry Redknapp

Premier League Review

The 2009/10 season will live long in the memory of all Spurs fans. A fourth placed finish guaranteed a Champions League qualifying place and the opportunity to pit our wits against the best clubs in Europe. Throughout the season the players maintained the consistency which was required in the race for fourth. We were in the top four for the majority of the season and victories over Arsenal, Chelsea and then Manchester City clinched Champions League football.

Champions League here we come!

August
Pld: 4 W: 4 D: 0 L: 0
End of month Position: 2nd

We started the season with a superb 2-1 win over title contenders Liverpool. An outstanding strike from Benoit Assou-Ekotto gave us the lead. Steven Gerrard levelled from the penalty spot. However, three minutes later Sebastien Bassong's header on his debut gave us all three points. Three days later we travelled to Hull City full of confidence and it showed as we played some sublime football on the way to winning 5-1. Jermain Defoe scored a stunning hat-trick with Wilson Palacios and Robbie Keane completing the rout. Our next away game was a London Derby against West Ham. Carlton Cole gave the home side the lead but a Jermain Defoe goal levelled the score. Three points were secured after Aaron Lennon's shot from outside the area found the bottom left hand corner to record yet another win over West Ham. Spurs were top of the Premier League after this result.

Our fourth successive league win came against an impressive Birmingham side. Peter Crouch scored on 72 minutes to give us the lead but Lee Bowyer's goal on 75 minutes looked to have secured a point for Alex McCleish's side. But in stoppage time Aaron Lennon again proved to be the match winner with the late goal. Spurs fans were in dreamland, what a start to the season. The one low point of the month was Luka Modric suffering a broken leg which would keep him out for four months.

September
Pld: 3 W: 1 D: 0 L: 2
End of month Position: 4th

Manchester United were the visitors in our next match. An over-head kick by Jermain Defoe gave us the lead but goals from Ryan Giggs, Anderson and Wayne Rooney ensured a comfortable win for the reigning Champions. We travelled to Chelsea next in what was to be our second defeat of the

season. An injury to Ledley King on 48 minutes seemed to affect the team as we were beaten 3-0. We bounced back in style as we beat newly-promoted Burnley 5-0. Robbie Keane scored four goals with Jermaine Jenas adding another to push us back into fourth place.

October
Pld: 4 W: 1 D: 1 L: 2
End of month Position: 4th

We travelled to the Reebok Stadium, Bolton at the beginning of the month. A Vedran Corluka header salvaged a point as we drew 2-2 in a match where Niko Kranjcar scored his first goal for the club. Our next match saw us travel south to Portsmouth. Goals from Jermain Defoe and Ledley King saw us on our way to a 2-1 victory. Defoe was later sent off in what was our only red card of the season. The month would end in disappointing fashion as we were beaten 1-0 against Stoke at The Lane and suffer a 3-0 defeat to Arsenal. Our early season form preserved 4th place.

November
Pld: 3 W: 2 D: 1 L: 0
End of month Position: 3rd

We were back to winning ways with a 2-0 win over Sunderland. Robbie Keane and a stunning strike from Tom Huddlestone were enough to ensure victory. The next match will be remembered for many years to come. Jermain Defoe hit five goals in our biggest win in over 30 years as we beat Wigan 9-1 at the Lane! Turn to Page 56 to re-live the amazing day. We travelled to play Aston Villa in buoyant mood after our demolition of Wigan. We returned with a point after Michael Dawson's excellent strike but in truth we deserved so much more after dominating for 80 minutes. We finished an amazing month in the top three.

December

Pld: 6 W: 3 D: 2 L: 1
End of month Position: 4th

Everton were our next opponents as we looked to build on our great early season form. A point would usually be a satisfactory result at Goodison Park but this turned out to be two points dropped as not only did we give away a two goal lead, Jermain Defoe missed a last minute penalty. Defoe and Michael Dawson were on target. Newly-promoted Wolves were next up and an early Kevin Doyle goal was enough to give Mick McCarthy's side all three points in a hugely frustrating game. One bright note was the return of Luka Modric after a broken leg. We returned to winning ways with a 3-0 demolition of Manchester City. Niko Kranjcar (2) and Jermain Defoe with the goals.

Blackburn at Ewood Park were our next opponents. A Peter Crouch double secured a hard-fought victory. On Boxing Day we travelled to Fulham. Neither side could break the deadlock and a point was a fair result. West Ham visited the Lane two days

later. Luka Modric and Jermain Defoe were on target as we strengthened our position in the top four.

January

Pld: 4 W: 1 D: 2 L: 1
End of month Position: 4th

Our first league game of 2010 saw us frustrated by Hull City at White Hart Lane in a 0-0 draw. As the race for fourth continued a 2-0 defeat at Liverpool was a setback. Jermain Defoe had a goal wrongly disallowed. We bounced back with a 2-0 win over Fulham. David Bentley and Peter Crouch with the goals. January ended with a 1-1 draw at Birmingham, Jermain Defoe putting us in front but a late Liam Ridgewell goal saw us leave Birmingham with only a point.

February

Pld: 4 W: 2 D: 1 L: 1
End of month Position: 4th

We were held to a goalless draw at home to Aston Villa as the battle for fourth was hotting up with Villa, Man City and Liverpool chasing that all important place.

Wolves got the better of us once again as we were defeated 1-0 at Molineux in one of our disappointing performances of the season.

Our first league win of the month came at the JJB Stadium as we defeated Wigan 3-0. Jermain Defoe and a double from Roman Pavlyuchenko sealed an impressive victory. We finished the month with a hard-fought win over Everton. Roman Pavlyuchenko continued his great run of league and cup form with a goal and a superb Luka Modric effort gave us a 2-0 half-time lead. Yakubu was on target in the second half but Spurs held on.

March
Pld: 3 W: 3 D: 0 L: 0
End of month Position: 4th

A double from Roman Pavlyuchenko and another from Jermain Defoe saw us beat Blackburn 3-1. A trip to Stoke is never an easy match but goals from Eidur Gudjohnsen and Niko Kranjcar secured victory in a determined performance.

Kranjcar was on target again as we beat Portsmouth 2-0 at White Hart Lane. Peter Crouch scored the other goal against Avram Grant's side.

April
Pld: 4 W: 2 D: 0 L: 2
End of month Position: 4th

With seven games remaining every point was crucial. Sadly the month didn't start well in a crazy game at Sunderland. Darren Bent scored two goals, one a penalty, Heurelho Gomes saved two further Darren Bent penalties, Peter Crouch got one back before the home side stopped a comeback in its tracks with a spectacular third.

The next league match was simply unforgettable. Tottenham 2-1 Arsenal, all but ending their hopes of winning the Premier League and a win which boosted our own chances of qualifying for the Champions League. A night to remember at White Hart Lane. Three days later, another derby, another win. Jermain Defoe and Gareth Bale completed a dream week in the Premier League as we deservedly beat Chelsea. Not only did we beat the eventual champions, we restored our place in the top four after Manchester City's defeat to United earlier in the day.

Our final match of the month completed our set of consecutive fixtures against the top three. Sadly this proved one game too many as Manchester United kept their title hopes alive with a 3-1 win.

May
Pld: 3 W: 2 D: 0 L: 1
Final Position: 4th

Tom Huddlestone's first half thunderbolt was enough to give us three points in a massive 1-0 victory over Bolton at the Lane in our final home game of the season. It was simple - beat Manchester City and we would qualify for the Champions League. A draw would take it into the final game and defeat would give City the advantage. Manager Harry Redknapp went with an attacking line-up that included Aaron Lennon, with Bale on the left-flank as a supply line for Jermain Defoe and Peter Crouch. We enjoyed the greater possession in the first half. Ledley King had a header ruled out for a foul. The decision looked harsh and left all Spurs fans wondering if we would look back on that incident if the night didn't turn out as we would hope. The second half saw Spurs create numerous chances, Defoe especially going close with on-loan 'keeper Marton Fulop making a string of fine saves. The goal our performance merited finally

arrived with eight minutes left as Crouch pounced after Fulop was unable to hold Younes Kaboul's cross. Tottenham now had ten minutes to defend for their lives. However, it was Spurs who created more chances in the final few minutes. The final whistle brought sheer elation from players and fans alike, with the whole squad off the bench and straight over to the travelling thousands. Fourth place was secure and now the chance to earn that Champions League jackpot.

Our final game of the season saw a tired looking Spurs side suffer defeat at relegated Burnley. Gareth Bale and a superb Luka Modric goal gave us a 2-0 lead. Burnley came back to record a deserved win. Even a final day defeat couldn't dampen the spirits of the travelling support. All in all after 38 games we thoroughly deserve our opportunity to play in Europe's premier club competition. The football at times was scintillating. The 'maybe next year' quote from many Spurs supporters no longer needs to be mentioned. We did it, and in style!

Final Premier League Table

	P	HW	HD	HL	HGF	HGA	AW	AD	AL	AGF	AGA	Points	GD
Chelsea	38	17	1	1	68	14	10	4	5	35	18	86	+71
Man Utd	38	16	1	2	52	12	11	3	5	34	16	85	+58
Arsenal	38	15	2	2	48	15	8	4	7	35	26	75	+42
Tottenham	**38**	**14**	**2**	**3**	**40**	**12**	**7**	**5**	**7**	**27**	**29**	**70**	**+26**
Man City	38	12	4	3	41	20	6	9	4	32	25	67	+28
Aston Villa	38	8	8	3	29	16	9	5	5	23	23	64	+13
Liverpool	38	13	3	3	43	15	5	6	8	18	20	63	+26
Everton	38	11	6	2	35	21	5	7	7	25	28	61	+11
Birmingham	38	8	9	2	19	13	5	2	12	19	34	50	-9
Blackburn	38	10	6	3	28	18	3	5	11	13	37	50	-14
Stoke	38	7	6	6	24	21	4	8	7	10	27	47	-14
Fulham	38	11	3	5	27	15	1	7	11	12	31	46	-7
Sunderland	38	9	7	3	32	19	2	4	13	16	37	44	-8
Bolton	38	6	6	7	26	31	4	3	12	16	36	39	-25
Wolves	38	5	6	8	13	22	4	5	10	19	34	38	-24
Wigan	38	6	7	6	19	24	3	2	14	18	55	36	-42
West Ham	38	7	5	7	30	29	1	6	12	17	37	35	-19
Burnley	38	7	5	7	25	30	1	1	17	17	52	30	-40
Hull	38	6	6	7	22	29	0	6	13	12	46	30	-41
Portsmouth*	38	5	3	11	24	32	2	4	13	10	34	19	-32

*Portsmouth deducted nine points for entering administration

FA Cup Review

Spurs appeared at Wembley for the third season in a row, this time for the FA Cup Semi-Final against Portsmouth. Despite a heartbreaking extra-time defeat, our elimination from the tournament gave the players the impetus to finish in the top four of the Premier League which was always the number one target.

FA Cup 3rd Round
TOTTENHAM HOTSPUR 4 - 0 PETERBOROUGH UNITED

Niko Kranjcar struck twice in a Man of the Match display as Harry Redknapp's men put Peterborough United to the sword in the FA Cup Third Round at the Lane. Jermain Defoe and Robbie Keane also got on the scoresheet in a one-sided 4-0 defeat of the Championship's bottom club.

FA Cup 4th Round
TOTTENHAM HOTSPUR 2-2 LEEDS UNITED

Jermaine Beckford dispatched a stoppage-time penalty to earn League One Leeds a replay and cap a sensational FA Cup fourth-round tie at White Hart Lane. We looked to have avoided becoming the victims of another upset at the hands of the League One leaders when Roman Pavlyuchenko came off the bench to hit what appeared to be the winner 20 minutes from time. But Beckford, Leeds' match-winner in their famous Third Round win against Manchester United at Old Trafford three weeks earlier, won and then slotted home a spot kick for his second of the game deep into injury time. He had earlier cancelled out Peter Crouch's opener, while Jermain Defoe saw a ninth minute penalty of his own saved.

FA Cup
4th Round Replay
LEEDS UNITED 1-3 TOTTENHAM HOTSPUR

A Jermain Defoe hat-trick at Elland Road saw the team to a 3-1 victory over Leeds United in an exciting FA Cup fourth round replay. Leeds did level just before the break in what was an absorbing contest, but the team asserted control in the second half and a further two goals did justice to a fine performance that booked us a trip to Bolton in round five of the competition.

FA Cup 5th Round
BOLTON 1-1 TOTTENHAM HOTSPUR

Tottenham fought back to earn an FA Cup fifth-round replay after an entertaining draw against Bolton. The hosts were much the better side in the first half and went ahead when Kevin Davies completed an impressive passing move by firing in on the turn. But Spurs responded and equalised when Jermain Defoe fired home on 61 minutes. And Tom Huddlestone spurned the chance to send Spurs through as Jussi Jaaskelainen saved his penalty after a Sam Ricketts handball.

FA Cup
5th Round Replay
TOTTENHAM HOTSPUR 4-0 BOLTON

Roman Pavlyuchenko continued his resurgence with two more goals to earn Tottenham an all-London FA Cup quarter-final away to Fulham. Jussi Jaaskelainen was at fault for the first of two Bolton own goals, the ball deflecting in off his leg as he failed to deal with a Wilson Palacios centre. Gareth Bale's cross later went in off Andrew O'Brien in a dominant performance.

FA Cup 6th Round
FULHAM 0-0 TOTTENHAM HOTSPUR

For the second time this season it finished goalless down by the Thames - this time in the FA Cup quarter-final - and we had to play it again at the Lane for a place at Wembley in the semi-finals. It was a contest of few clear opportunities, Heurelho Gomes making the most athletic save on the stretch in a game where his central defenders stood tall and Wilson Palacios in front of them gave a typically all-action, combative - yet very disciplined performance.

FA Cup
6th Round Replay
TOTTENHAM HOTSPUR 3-1 FULHAM

Inspired substitutions from Harry Redknapp turned our FA Cup Quarter-Final replay with Fulham on its head to send us through to the Wembley semis. Trailing 1-0 at the break, David Bentley was introduced and equalised with his first touch before Roman Pavlyuchenko also came off the bench to score one of the goals of the season to send us on our way.

In a 20 minute spell at the start of the second half, our astonishing comeback was completed when the impressive Eidur Gudjohnsen made it two goals in as many games to settle the tie.

FA Cup Semi-Final
TOTTENHAM HOTSPUR 0-2 PORTSMOUTH (AFTER EXTRA-TIME)

Our FA Cup dreams faded as a combination of missed chances, last-ditch defending and that little slice of luck against us saw Portsmouth claim an FA Cup Final place. Few would argue that we should have wrapped up this encounter before Fredrique Piquionne finally broke the deadlock in the first half of extra time. Chances came and went, David James produced saves when it mattered and then, crucially, Michael Dawson suffered the misfortune of slipping at the key moment on the controversial Wembley pitch, allowing Piquionne the opportunity from six yards in the 99th minute. That was a real hammer blow but even then, within seconds of the goal, we were straight up the other end only for Peter Crouch to hit the post and then see a goal disallowed as referee Alan Wiley blew the whistle for a foul by Niko Kranjcar on James. We couldn't find a goal in the second half of extra time and Pompey wrapped it up from the penalty spot in the 117th minute, Kevin-Prince Boateng drilling home following Wilson Palacios' foul on Aruna Dindane. Defeat meant our sole aim for the season was Champions League football. The chase continued three days after this defeat against Arsenal in the Premier League.

Spurs: **Gomes; Corluka, Bassong, Dawson, Bale; Bentley (Kranjcar, 79), Huddlestone (Gudjohnsen, 101), Palacios, Modric; Crouch, Defoe (Pavlyuchenko, 59). Subs: Alnwick, Assou-Ekotto, Livermore, Rose.**

Carling Cup
Review

After two successive final appearances our 2009/10 Carling Cup adventure came to an end at eventual winners Manchester United in the Quarter-Finals as two Darron Gibson goals were enough to send Sir Alex Ferguson's side through.

2nd Round
DONCASTER 1-5 TOTTENHAM HOTSPUR

We started our 2009/10 Carling Cup campaign in the Second Round with a tricky looking tie at the Keepmoat Stadium but the players produced a thoroughly professional performance to comfortably beat the Championship side. Goals from Tom Huddlestone, Jamie O'Hara, Peter Crouch, David Bentley and Roman Pavlyuchenko secured the win. The likes of Kyle Naughton, Giovani Dos Santos and Danny Rose all featured as our superb early season form continued.

3rd Round
PRESTON 1-5 TOTTENHAM HOTSPUR

Peter Crouch scored a hat-trick as another 5-1 victory secured a fourth round place at the expense of Championship side Preston. Crouch and Defoe were on target to give us a 2-0 lead at half-time. Crouch added another before Chris Brown pulled a goal back. Robbie Keane made it 4-1 to Spurs. Two minutes into injury time Crouch scored his third with an audacious backheel. Once again, Harry Redknapp's team were showing a clinical edge that was beyond their opponents.

4th Round
TOTTENHAM HOTSPUR 2-0 EVERTON

Our good form in the Carling Cup continued with a hard-fought win over Everton. Tom Huddlestone and Robbie Keane booked a place in the quarter-finals at the Lane. Huddlestone hammered home a thunderous opener in the 31st minute and Keane doubled the tally just before the hour, following up at the third attempt after Tim Howard saved his initial penalty. Harry Redknapp was looking for our squad members to step up to the plate and he wasn't disappointed as Gareth Bale, Alan Hutton, David Bentley and Roman Pavlyuchenko all impressed - all it needed was the Russian hitman to score to complete the night.

5th Round
MANCHESTER UNITED 2-0 TOTTENHAM HOTSPUR

Our Carling Cup journey for season 2009-10 came to an end at Old Trafford when two first half goals from Darron Gibson proved enough for Manchester United to progress to the semi-final stage. Harry Redknapp made five changes to the team that started at Aston Villa three days prior to the United match, with Alan Hutton, Gareth Bale, David Bentley, Jermaine Jenas and Robbie Keane all drafted in. We arrived at Old Trafford full of optimism but in truth we created very little. United went on to retain the Carling Cup after beating Aston Villa 2-1.

Michael Dawson
Player of the year

At the end of season 2009/10 Michael Dawson was voted the One Hotspur Player of the Season, Boxholders Player of the Season and Supporters' Clubs Player of the Year. The popular central defender played a big part in our successful quest for Champions League football. His amazing season ended with a call-up to England's World Cup squad in South Africa.

Michael has been a key part of our back-line ever since his arrival from Nottingham Forest as a 21-year-old in January, 2005. He captained the side for much of the 2009/10 campaign. Dawson's form was not only recognised by Spurs supporters but was widely praised week in, week out from many media sources and his Tottenham Player of the Year Award was no surprise. "It's a special award for me because it comes from the Spurs fans who I love and who watch me every week. They've been good to me ever since I joined and I cherish that joint rapport. If they think I've had a good season then that's good enough for me and I thank them all. Everything we do we do for the supporters and I rate our followers as the best in the land."

Dawson's form last season saw him called up to Fabio Capello's initial 30-man World Cup squad. Originally, Michael missed out on the final 23-man squad but injury to Rio Ferdinand meant Michael was named as his replacement. Michael did not feature in England's hugely disappointing campaign but he has been widely tipped to be one of many new faces for England in their Euro 2012 qualifying campaign. "When you're playing for a top football club, as I have been on a regular basis and putting in good performances, there's always that chance of playing for England. Luckily enough, I got the call."

Michael missed the beginning of last season with an Achilles injury. He returned for the 9-1 hammering of Wigan in November and missed just one of our next 35 games. One week after our victory over Wigan, Michael scored a stunning equaliser to earn Spurs a draw at Aston Villa. He also scored a fine header in December away at Everton. 'Daws' also featured in both derby victories over Arsenal and Chelsea. Against Chelsea Michael made a last ditch tackle on Didier Drogba to preserve our lead. Such form led to the "Dawson for England" chant from the Spurs supporters. Fabio Capello was clearly listening. It is amazing to think Michael had yet to receive an England cap after the World Cup but there is little doubt that if fit, he has the ability to become a firm fixture in the national side whilst continuing his superb career at Tottenham Hotspur.

Gareth Bale
Young player of the year

Gareth received the Club's Young Player of the Year award after an incredible second half of the 2009-10 campaign. Despite being out of the side in the early part of the season, his transformation was unbelievable, terrorising defences with his speed and strength down the left wing and also scoring in derby victories over Arsenal and Chelsea.

Gareth Bale joined Tottenham from Southampton in May 2007 after we beat off competition from a number of clubs. He got off to a great start at Spurs scoring three goals in 12 matches including a superb free-kick against Arsenal. Sadly, in December Bale suffered a broken foot which ended his maiden season prematurely. The following season Gareth featured in 16 games but the form of Benoit Assou-Ekotto meant the majority of Gareth's playing time came from the bench.

The beginning of last season saw Gareth miss the majority of matches due to injury and once again the form of Assou-Ekotto. However, an injury to Benoit at the turn of the year gave him his chance for a run of games, and he never looked back, earning Man of the Match awards and rave reviews throughout the remainder of the campaign.

Gareth made 34 appearances in total that season, scoring three Premier League goals which included valuable winners in our victories over Arsenal and Chelsea in April, 2010. By the end of last season, the young player of the year had been awarded with a new contract that will keep the precocious talent at the Lane until 2014. "It's always nice to receive an award from your own fans as they are the people who watch you every week," adds Bale, the recipient of our One Hotspur 'Young Player of the Year' award, together with a number of other accolades. "Our supporters have always been great to me and I really appreciate that because I rate them as the best around."

Manager Harry Redknapp will hope Gareth stays injury free in 2011 with Champions League football and another long Premier League season on the way. Despite his previous problems with injuries Manager Harry Redknapp was adamant Gareth will play a big role in the side. "It would have scared me to death to have sold him," said Redknapp. "I know what he can do. The sky is the limit for him."

Harry Redknapp

In his first full season in charge of Tottenham Hotspur Harry Redknapp has secured Champions League qualification for the club. It completes a remarkable turnaround as we were bottom of the table in October 2008 but are now competing at the very top of the league.

Harry said on the night of his shock appointment that it wouldn't take much to transform Spurs into a Champions League chasing side. But even Redknapp was surprised by the nature of our success. "It's been a pleasure to watch. I've enjoyed watching the lads play, with the way we move the ball around, because that's how I like to play and it's been fantastic."

Harry was also named the Barclays Manager of the Season. The award recognised our achievement by qualifying for the Champions League for the first time. "I was delighted to receive the award but it's a team effort with Kevin (Bond), Joe (Jordan), Clive (Allen), Tony (Parks), Tim (Sherwood), Les (Ferdinand) and all the coaching and fitness staff. Really, I'm just part of the team. It's all down to the players and what they've achieved. It's down to them really but I'm honoured to receive it."

Perhaps Harry's biggest achievement was enabling Spurs to play well on a consistent basis. They have always recorded memorable results but the lack of successive victories often led the club to miss out on lucrative league finishes. However, victories at places like Blackburn, Stoke and West Ham combined with memorable wins over Arsenal, Chelsea and Manchester City saw us secure a top four finish.

Typically, Harry has already moved on from last season as he plans another dramatic season ahead at White Hart Lane. He realises success creates bigger challenges as we look to consolidate our place among the elite of English football. "It will be exciting but very tough. The usual three will be up there again and you have to think Manchester City will be even stronger. Liverpool will improve under Roy Hodgson and I'm also expecting big things from Aston Villa and Everton so we know it's going to be hard."

Harry is looking forward to the prospect of managing a club in the Champions League for the first time but is fully aware that a good start in the league will shape the entire season. "We started last season in the right way and didn't look back. We proved we could play against anyone."

Off the pitch, his conduct with the media and his sense of humour have helped make Harry a national treasure. One of the lasting memories from season 2009/10 will undoubtedly be the players drenching Harry in iced-cold water during a post match interview with Sky Sports following our win at Manchester City. He might not admit it, but Harry will probably accept the same fate again at the end of the season if it's something to celebrate.

Player profiles
2010/2011

Heurelho Gomes ▶

The Brazilian International enjoys a great rapport with Spurs fans and is now in his third season at the club. His form last season played a huge part in our successful chase for Champions League football. Gomes's three world class saves against Arsenal at The Lane will live long in the memory.

Vedran Corluka ▼

Super-consistent Croatian international full-back, Vedran started 29 of our first 30 games in the Premier League until injury ended his campaign early. Now in his third season at the club, 'Charlie' continues to be our first-choice right-back.

Carlo Cudicini ▲

Carlo joined Spurs from Chelsea in January 2009. He has provided strong competition for the Number One jersey. In November, 2009, Carlo sustained injuries to his wrists and pelvis in a road accident, cutting his season short. But by the end of the 2009-10 campaign, he had returned to training and was awarded a new one-year contract at the Club to continue his recovery. He was back in action in pre-season.

Gareth Bale ▼

Gareth's breathtaking form from January 2010 earned him a new contract at the end of the season. He scored in both derby victories against Arsenal and Chelsea. The powerful left-sided Welsh international was awarded the Club's Young Player of the Year award after an incredible second half of the 2009-10 campaign.

Younes Kaboul ▲

The athletic defender rejoined the Club from Portsmouth in January, 2010. Younes had left White Hart Lane for Fratton Park 18 months earlier having originally arrived from French club Auxerre in July, 2007. Younes provided the assist for Peter Crouch's crucial goal at Manchester City last season.

William Gallas ▶

The France international was part of the Chelsea side that won back-to-back Premier League titles as well as the League Cup in 2005. His performances during Chelsea's second Premier League-winning campaign saw him included in the 2005/06 PFA Premier League Team of the Year.
The former Caen and Marseille defender left Stamford Bridge after five seasons, during which he made 213 appearances and scored 14 goals, to join Arsenal in September 2006. Gallas captained the side during the 2007/08 campaign and went on to make 145 appearances, scoring 17 goals before leaving at the end of last season.

Michael Dawson ▼

The popular defender capped-off a superb 2009/10 season with a place in Fabio Capello's 23-man England squad. His form earned a number of awards including One Hotspur Player of the Season, Boxholders Player of the Season and Supporters' Clubs Player of the Year.

Kyle Walker ▲

Kyle enjoyed an impressive pre-season for Spurs which put him firmly in the first team picture for 2011. The England Under-19 international joined us from Sheffield United, along with fellow young defender Kyle Naughton, in July 2009. He was subsequently loaned back to The Blades to gain further first team experience for the 2009/2010 campaign. He made his Spurs debut against Portsmouth in March, 2010.

Ledley King ▶

The Spurs club captain is the longest-serving member of our playing staff, Ledley's performances at the end of the 2009-10 campaign earned a place in England's World Cup squad. A classy, stylish defender who reads the game so well and will relish leading us into the Champions League.

Sebastien Bassong ▼

Strong central defender joined us from Newcastle United in August, 2009. 'Seb' scored on his debut against Liverpool on the opening day of the season. Bassong featured in Cameroon's 2010 World Cup campaign.

David Bentley ▲

David's ability is beyond question and re-discovered his form last season. Injury to Aaron Lennon gave David the opportunity to play an important role in the side. The likeable winger was the main culprit for throwing iced water over Harry Redknapp after our 1-0 win over Manchester City!

Benoit Assou-Ekotto ▶

Benoit scored our first goal of last season against Liverpool. Like Bassong he featured in Cameroon's 2010 World Cup campaign. His consistency at left-back has allowed Gareth Bale to play a more advanced role in the side.

Tom Huddlestone ▼

Last season saw Tom play a key role in our successful league campaign. Tom started more Premier League games than anyone else (33/38) and made more starts (41/50) in all competitions than anyone apart from goalkeeper Heurelho Gomes, who made 42. His form earned a call into Fabio Capello's provisional 30-man World Cup squad, but he was unfortunately cut from the final 23.

Jermaine Jenas ▲

This is Jermaine's sixth season at the club and is now one of the longest-serving players at the club. An experienced campaigner in a central midfield, JJ made 23 appearances including 13 starts in all competitions in 2009-10.

Aaron Lennon ▶

The lightning England international winger was in the form of his life before his 2009-10 campaign was cut short by injury. He scored back-to-back winners against Birmingham and West Ham and bagged a number of assists as he started 18 of our first 20 matches. However, a groin problem then got the better of him in late December and he didn't return to action until April 24. His form over the campaign was enough for inclusion into Fabio Capello's World Cup squad - his second World Cup Finals at the age of 23.

Jamie O'Hara ▼

The midfielder impressed on loan at Portsmouth in 2009-10, culminating in an FA Cup Final appearance against Chelsea. Jamie fulfilled his lifelong dream of breaking into our First Team in December 2007, having come through the Club's Academy.

Luka Modric ▲

Luka's world-class performances were pivotal in key wins against Arsenal, Chelsea and Manchester City as we finished fourth in the Premier League. Having started the season well, he suffered a fractured fibula against Birmingham City in August and didn't return until December. He went on to make 32 appearances in all competitions, starting 21 matches in the Premier League, scoring three goals. At the end of the season Luka signed a new six-year contract which runs until 2016.

Wilson Palacios ▶

Wilson was a key signing as we tried to move away from the bottom half of the table in January 2009. The Honduran international started 29 matches in the Premier League and made 37 appearances in all competitions before jetting off to the World Cup in South Africa.

Niko Kranjcar ▼

The Croatian international's excellent first season in 2009-10 was unfortunately cut short by injury sustained in the FA Cup semi-final at Wembley in April. But he made quite an impact in his 29 appearances in all competitions, scoring eight goals including spectacular hits against Peterborough United, Stoke and against Manchester City at the Lane when he beat Emmanuel Adebayor all ends up before slotting home. Niko joined us from Portsmouth on transfer deadline day in September 2009.

Jermain Defoe ▲

Our top-scorer in 2009-10, Jermain made history during the season before joining an elite Spurs club by scoring for England at the World Cup Finals in June. Jermain became only the third player in Premier League history to score five goals in a match when he achieved the feat in the 9-1 defeat of Wigan in November. Defoe scored 24 goals in all competitions, helping fire us to fourth place in the Premier League.

Robbie Keane ▶

Robbie was the fifteenth player in Spurs' history to reach the 100 goal landmark. Ninth in our all-time goalscoring list, the popular Irish striker spent the second half of the 2009-10 season on loan to Celtic. Robbie, the Republic's skipper and all-time top goalscorer, bagged 16 goals in 19 appearances at Celtic Park.

Roman Pavlyuchenko ▼

The Russian International is a crowd favourite. 'Super Pav' enjoyed a purple patch of eight goals in eight games in February and March of the 2009-10 season. That spell was the highlight for the striker as a combination of injuries and the form of our other strikers restricted 'Pav' to 26 appearances and only 12 starts in all competitions, scoring 10 goals.

Giovani Dos Santos ▲

'Gio' returns to Spurs after spending five months on loan at Galatasaray. Injuries again halted the young Mexican's progress at the Lane in 2009-10. Dos Santos recently caught the eye at the 2010 World Cup in South Africa where his Mexico side reached the Last 16.

Peter Crouch ▶

England international striker who will go down in Spurs history as the man who scored the goal that took us into the Champions League. That came at Manchester City on May 5, 2010, when 'Crouchy' headed home from close range to secure a 1-0 win and fourth place in the Premier League. The goal proved 'lucky' number 13 for the season after Peter made an impressive 46 appearances out of a possible 50 in all competitions, starting 29.

Champions league here we come!

Wednesday May 5th will live long in the memory of all Tottenham supporters. The young generation have often been told by their parents of the 'Glory Glory' nights for Spurs and this one is right up there as a Peter Crouch header was enough to secure Champions League football at Manchester City.

Derby Delight

After a 2-0 defeat to Portsmouth in the FA Cup Semi-Final Tottenham were fifth in the Premier League. Champions League football now looked an unlikely prospect after such a disappointing defeat at Wembley. The players didn't have long to prepare for two of the biggest derby matches in recent history.

Tottenham Hotspur 2-1 Arsenal
April 14th, 2010

It was impossible to put into words the significance of this win. Just three days after the disappointment of an unexpected FA Cup semi-final defeat came the result of the season so far bar none.

Our first league victory over our arch rivals since November 1999. One that kept our quest for a top four finish well and truly on track. Not only did it help our chances of Champions League football it also ended Arsenal's title hopes.

Before the match not a single Spurs fan would've predicted that 19-year-old Danny Rose, on his debut at this level, would score the goal of the season to set us on our way to a 2-1 victory. Two minutes into the second half it was 2-0.

Gareth Bale, the Premier League's best player after January with the goal that gave us a healthy lead. Arsenal as expected piled on the pressure, Gomes had to make three world class saves to preserve our two goal lead. Nicklas Bendtner's late strike made it an unbearably tense finish but we held on. The final whistle was greeted with such ecstasy, and with every good reason.

Spurs (4-4-2): **Gomes; Kaboul, Dawson, King, Assou-Ekotto; Rose (Bentley, 46), Huddlestone, Modric, Bale; Defoe (Gudjohnsen, 68), Pavlyuchenko (Crouch, 88)** Subs not used: **Alnwick, Bassong, K Walker, Livermore**

Arsenal (4-3-3): **Almunia; Sagna (Walcott, 53), Campbell, Vermaelen (Silvestre, 20), Clichy; Denilson (Van Persie, 68), Nasri, Diaby; Eboue, Rosicky, Bendtner** Subs not used: **Fabianski, Eastmond, Merida, Eduardo**

Tottenham Hotspur 2-1 Chelsea
April 17th, 2010

After putting Arsenal to the sword, few pundits gave the lads a chance of repeating the trick against the leaders and title favourites. But this was an even better display as we completed a dream week in the Premier League deservedly beating Chelsea to move back into fourth place. We'd built up a head of steam and were rewarded in the 15th minute as referee Phil Dowd pointed to the spot when David Bentley's cross appeared to strike John Terry's arm. Jermain Defoe had missed his last two spot kicks against Leeds and Everton but didn't shirk the responsibility - this time he went with power and almost took the net off for 1-0, a deserved lead. We continued to dominate the game, the second goal was always going to be vital and Gareth Bale was there to deliver. This time, Pavlyuchenko played the perfect pass in behind Ferreira and Bale got onto the ball, cut inside the full-back and drilled home with his right foot. Defensively intact and marshalled superbly by Michael Dawson, Chelsea didn't seriously threaten in the second half and when Terry was sent off for a second yellow card in the 67th minute, it was all Spurs. It really could have been a cricket score but a combination of wayward finishing and the brilliance of Petr Cech kept it to 2-0.

Hearts were in mouths for a few moments when Frank Lampard slid home for 2-1 in the second minute of added time but, thankfully, we held on.

And with United beating City in the Manchester derby, it was the perfect day in terms of the fight for fourth place - we completed it in fourth, two points ahead of City. FA Cup heartache was forgotten inside a week as we made it a derby double to remember.

Spurs (4-4-2): **Gomes; Kaboul, Bassong, Dawson, Assou-Ekotto; Bentley, Huddlestone, Modric, Bale; Defoe (Gudjohnsen, 77), Pavlyuchenko.** Subs: **Alnwick, K Walker, Livermore, Rose, Townsend, Crouch.**

Chelsea: **Cech; Ferreira (Ivanovic, 46), Terry, Alex, Zhirkov; Malouda, Deco, Mikel (Ballack, 33), Lampard, J Cole (Anelka, 46); Drogba.** Subs: **Hilario, A Cole, Kalou, Sturridge.**

Who am I?

Can you identify the Spurs players below?

A

B

BENTLEY

GOMES

C

D

DEFOE

CROUCH

Answers p58

Wordsearch

Can you find the names of TEN Spurs players in this wordsearch? Words can go horizontally, vertically and diagonally.

```
C O R L U K A Q H B E H C A B
F U F H R Y P R S D O U M L V
H F G G D T E W E G S D V S X
J F H N I A B C W A B D Y N M
K V J V D K W X M P T L I V G
G L A M J E L S L X M E R H Z
U E O L X I F X O Y D S S A L
F N P H G C A O A N S T D L I
S N F M Q A I Q E N E O M I T
M O D R I C W R A Y D N N W V
D N G C G F N K Z P E E N Z T
C E O K Q E U L B O T A H R I
B D M P B B B B A C R O U C H
O C E H M I N Y L U K M U I I
B Y S T O M N F E J B K I N G
```

GOMES
BALE
CORLUKA
KING
DAWSON

MODRIC
HUDDLESTONE
LENNON
DEFOE
CROUCH

Answers p58

Pre-season Review

Tottenham enjoyed another entertaining pre-season. With many key players returning late from World Cup duty, the likes of Kyle Walker and Kyle Naughton were given the opportunity to impress while Giovani Dos Santos & Robbie Keane's impressive form saw them become an important part of Harry Redknapp's first team plans at the start of the season.

Bournemouth 0-4 Tottenham

Roman Pavlyuchenko scored two as we opened pre-season with a 4-0 win at Harry Redknapp's former club. Jon Obika and Danny Rose were also on the scoresheet as we dominated against the League One side.

San Jose Earthquakes 0-0 Tottenham

The first pre-season contest of our USA programme ended all square against San Jose Earthquakes. A record 10,712 in attendance witnessed an entertaining draw against our club partners.

New York Red Bulls 1-2 Tottenham

Robbie Keane and Gareth Bale scored the goals that got us off to a winning start in the Barclays New York Challenge against New York Red Bulls.

Sporting Lisbon 2-2 Tottenham

The USA leg of our pre-season preparations concluded with a 2-2 draw against Sporting Lisbon in the Barclays New York Challenge. Robbie Keane opened the scoring with his second goal in two games before Sporting hit back with a goal either side of half-time. Jon Obika secured a share of the spoils with 20 minutes remaining.

Tottenham 1-4 Villarreal

An impressive Villarreal put us to the sword in the first of two home friendlies at White Hart Lane this summer. Giovani Dos Santos scored our only goal.

Benfica 0-1 Tottenham

The team won the Eusebio Cup courtesy of a 1-0 victory over Benfica in our penultimate pre-season game in Lisbon. Gareth Bale scored the second half goal that saw the cup head back to London, the previous editions having been won by Inter Milan and the hosts Benfica.

Tottenham 3-2 Fiorentina

Robbie Keane scored a late winner in our final pre-season match. Keane earlier equalised while Roman Pavlyuchenko gave us an early lead.

PLAYER DEVELOPMENT COURSES

TOTTENHAM HOTSPUR™

FOOTBALL DEVELOPMENT

LEARN TO PLAY WITH TOTTENHAM HOTSPUR AND OUR TEAM OF FA QUALIFIED AND ACADEMY COACHES

COME AND JOIN US AT OUR SOCCER SCHOOLS IN HERTFORDSHIRE, ESSEX AND KENT RUNNING THROUGHOUT THE SCHOOL HOLIDAYS

OR FIND US ON ONE OF OUR NATIONWIDE ROADSHOWS RUNNING THROUGHOUT THE YEAR

FOR MORE INFORMATION OR TO BOOK CALL 0208 365 5049 OR ONLINE AT TOTTENHAMHOTSPUR.COM

TO DARE IS TO DO™

TOTTENHAMHOTSPUR.COM

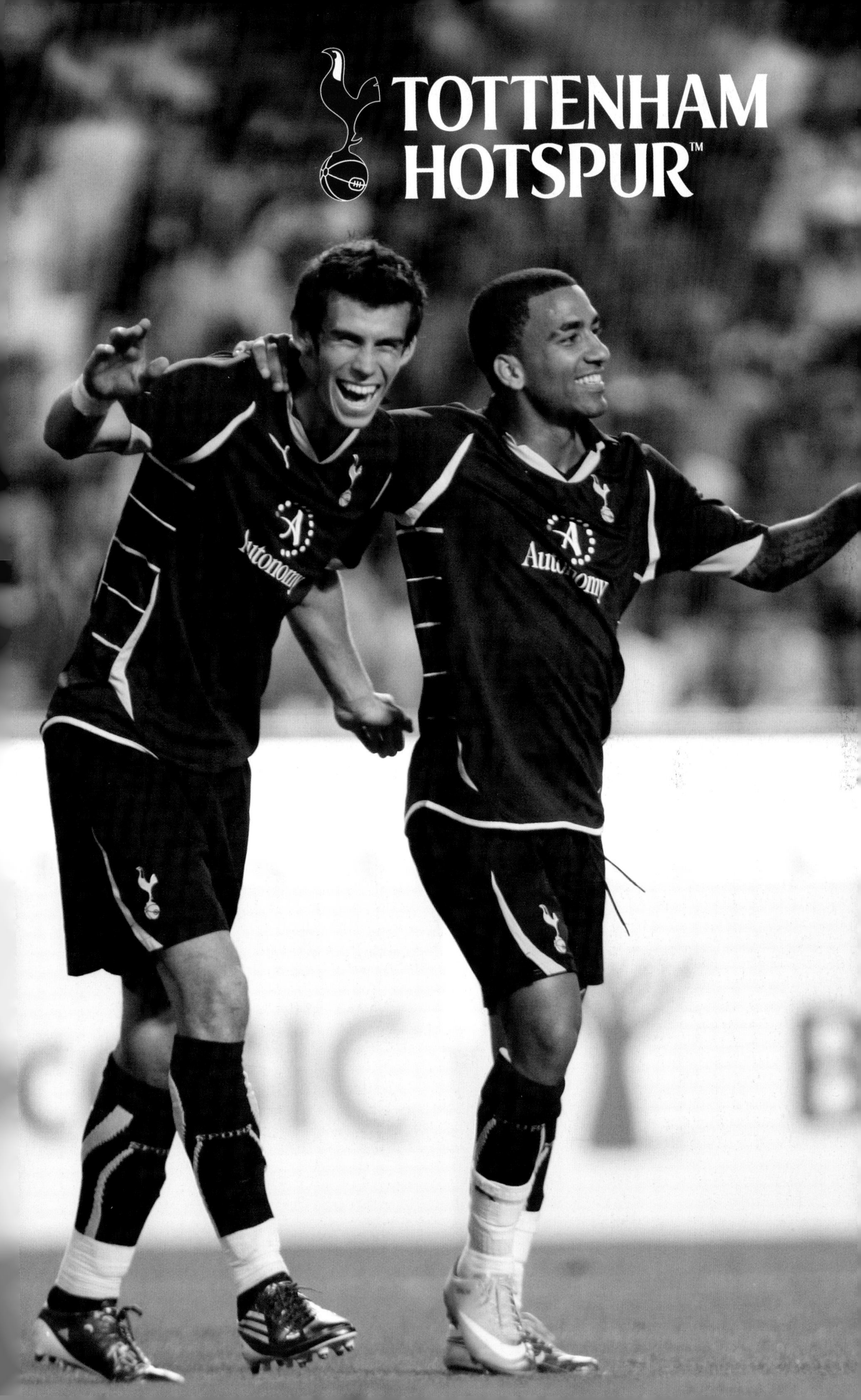
TOTTENHAM
HOTSPUR™
Autonomy
Autonomy

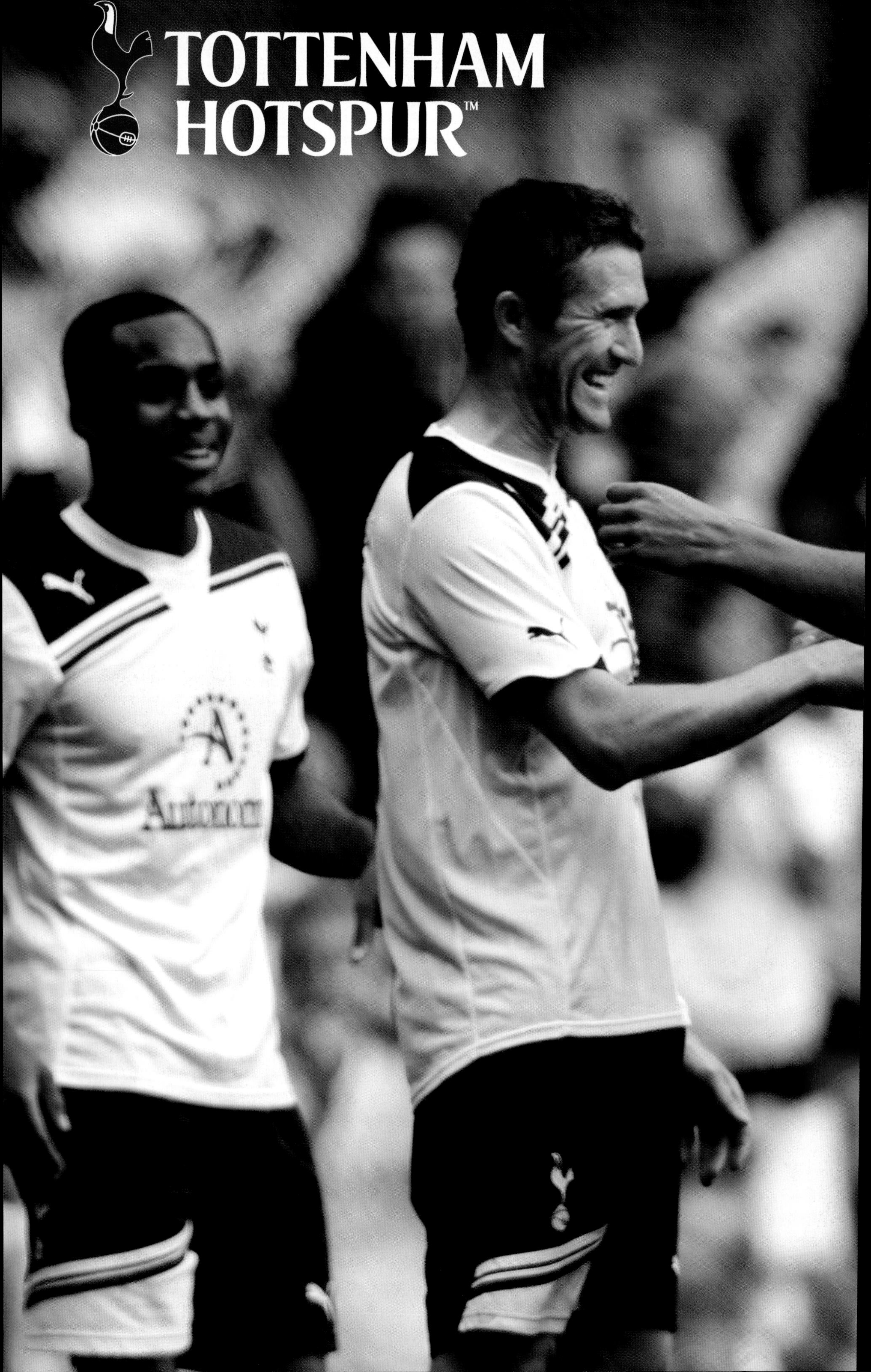
TOTTENHAM
HOTSPUR™

Super Spurs Quiz

It's a grand old team to play for and it's a grand old team to see, so if you know your history, try this 2011 Super Size Spurs Quiz

Q1 Where did Spurs finish last season?

> 4ts

Q2 Name our new Brazilian signing who plays in central midfield.

> Sandro

Q3 Who did we beat in the 2008 Carling Cup Final?

> Chelsea

Q4 Which player scored the crucial goal against Manchester City in May last season?

> Crouchy

Q5 Name the five Spurs players who featured in the England World Cup squad.

> Ryce, Dawson, King, Lennon, Crouch

Q6 How many goals did Jermain Defoe score in our 9-1 win over Wigan last season?

> 5

Q7 Name the two former Argentinean International's who joined Spurs in 1978.

> O. Ardiles, Villa

Q8 Harry Redknapp joined Spurs from which club?

> Portsmouth

Q9 True or false...Tottenham were formed by boys from a cricket club?

> True

Q10 Who captained Spurs to the 1991 FA Cup Final?

> Gary Mabutt

Q11 Which nation does Wilson Palacios represent?

> Honduras

Q12 Who scored our second goal in the 2-1 win over Arsenal last season?

> Bale

Q13 Gareth Bale joined Spurs from which club in 2007?

> Southampton

Q14 Which Croatian International signed a new six-year contract in the Summer?

> Modric

Q15 How many league goals did Jermain Defoe score last season?

> 24

Answers p58

Kevin Bond

Every great Manager needs a good backroom team and Harry Redknapp made sure he had his close friend Kevin Bond alongside him at Tottenham Hotspur.

Born in West Ham, London, Kevin started his football career as an apprentice at Bournemouth before returning for a second spell as a seasoned professional in 1988 and then managing the club between 2006-08.

When his father and Bournemouth's then-manager John moved on in 1974, Kevin went with him to Norwich City - and his career flourished.

He went on to play for Norwich, Manchester City and Southampton, racking up almost 400 appearances in the top flight and winning two England B caps in 1979-80. His playing career went full circle with a return to Bournemouth in 1988 - managed by none other than Harry Redknapp - and he made 126 league appearances before a short spell at Exeter and then ending his career in non-league.

Kevin followed in his father's footsteps by taking the managerial reins at Dean Court in 2006. Faced with a 10-point deduction, he almost kept the Cherries in League One in 2007-08. He then left to hook up again with Harry at Spurs.

Joe Jordan

Alongside Kevin Bond is another hugely valuable asset to Manager Harry Redknapp. Joe Jordan joined Spurs shortly after Redknapp's appointment and has been a key member of the backroom team ever since.

Joe played at the top level of the game for the majority of his 20-year career. Born in Carluke, Lanarkshire on December 15, 1951, Joe started his professional career with Greenock Morton aged 17 in 1968.

Joe joined Leeds United in 1970 and was soon representing Scotland. He was a physical striker with a great eye for goal. He would play alongside the likes of Billy Bremner, Allan Clarke and Mick Jones in Don Revie's side. Joe picked up a European Cup Winners Cup Runners-Up medal after Leeds were beaten 1-0 by AC Milan in 1973. The following season Joe scored nine goals in 25 games as Leeds won the First Division title. Jordan spent three years at Manchester United where he scored 37 goals in 109 games. After Old Trafford, Joe moved to AC Milan and proved to be a big hit scoring 12 goals in 52 games. After a brief spell at Verona Joe returned to England with Southampton, before ending his career as a player-manager at Bristol City.

Such playing experience makes him a great asset to Harry Redknapp. Joe is a very vocal coach on the touchline who gets his point across to the players. Harry Redknapp and his influence will continue to play an important role in the club's progress for seasons to come.

From the Academy to the Champions League!

Ledley King and Peter Crouch came through our Academy ranks together - now they've helped take the club into the Champions League.

Club skipper Ledley and striker 'Crouchy' both joined us full-time as Trainees in July, 1997 and turned professional in July, 1998.

Ledley captained the side and Crouchy scored the goal as a 1-0 win at Manchester City clinched fourth place in the Premier League and therefore a place in the Champions League next season.

Were they dreaming of such nights back in 1997?

"At that age you are just dreaming of becoming a professional footballer and that was our goal," said Ledley.

"Crouchy went onto different clubs and made

a name for himself elsewhere before coming back and it's fantastic he scored the goal at City. I was really pleased for him.

"Nights like that are very special and it's great we could share it together after being in the youth team here.

"This has been a long time coming - too long - and I'm delighted."

Crouchy added: "I'd rank this night up there with the best I've been a part of.

"I remember those Champions League nights when I was at Liverpool were so special and I can see them being just as special at White Hart Lane."

Spurs at the World Cup

We had ten Spurs players representing their respective countries in South Africa. We also had more players representing England than any other club. Jermain Defoe scored the vital goal for England against Slovenia. The team went out to Germany in the Last 16.

Jermain, Ledley King, Michael Dawson, Aaron Lennon and Peter Crouch were part of Fabio Capello's England squad. Tom Huddlestone also made the provisional World Cup squad but didn't make the final 23. However, Tom is likely to play a big part in future campaigns.

Heurelho Gomes was part of the Brazil Squad.

Sebastien Bassong and Benoit Assou-Ekotto both featured in the Cameroon squad.

Wilson Palacios represented Honduras.

Giovani dos Santos impressed for Mexico as they were eliminated in the Last 16.

Northumberland Development Project

The planning application for this world-class scheme has been submitted to Haringey Council.

This scheme incorporates a state-of-the-art 56,250 capacity stadium, a hotel, new homes, a supermarket, a new Club shop and museum, a new base for the Tottenham Hotspur Foundation and an exceptional new public square.

Our new state-of-the-art stadium has been designed to maximize atmosphere and features a new single tier stand.

The new Tottenham Hotspur Training Centre

Work has started on our new training centre in Enfield. This world class facility is due for completion in 2012.

The Centre will be the new home for the Club's First Team and Youth Academy training and provide an additional base for the Tottenham Hotspur Foundation, the Club's charity engaged in sport-related community work.

It is vital for the future success of the Club that we are able to attract, develop and retain the most talented, quality players and to develop youth players through the Academy. This new Training Centre will create exactly the environment in which to do this.

"Having come through the ranks here at Spurs and understanding the value and importance the Club places on developing home-grown talent, this facility will provide a fantastic platform for our Academy." Ledley King, Club Captain

Goal of the
Season

The official Spurs website once again asked supporters to vote online for their favourite goal of the season. We scored some superb goals as we secured fourth place in the Premier League but one goal in particular will stand out for years to come.

Benoit Assou-Ekotto v Liverpool

Sunday August 16, White Hart Lane

3rd

Benoit, a full-back who, after 151 professional appearances and no goals, was perhaps the most unlikely source from which we were to open our account for the season.

Assou-Ekotto's strike, however, was one even some of the most accomplished goal-getters would have been proud of. And what a time to get it, on the stroke of half-time, as Huddlestone's free-kick rebounded off the Liverpool wall, the Cameroon international took one touch before rifling an unstoppable 25 yard shot into Reina's top right-hand corner, sending the home crowd into raptures. It was our first goal of the season and what a way to get us off the mark!

Luka Modric v Everton

Sunday February 28, White Hart Lane

2nd

A world class goal from a world class player. An entertaining first half ended with a wonderful goal. It was all about our Croatian trio as Kranjcar, Modric and Corluka played the ball around in a tight space on the right. Eventually Kranjcar fed Modric on the right edge, he drove forward a couple of yards before somehow pinging a shot home off the underside of the crossbar.

And the winner is...

Danny Rose's amazing strike against Arsenal won the vote for our 2009/10 Goal of the Season

Wednesday April 14, White Hart Lane

It was hardly surprising that the 30-yard volley 10 minutes into the derby that set us on our way to a memorable 2-1 win over the Gunners gained 74 per cent of the vote.
It was a must win game for Tottenham. Just days after a heartbreaking FA Cup exit against Portsmouth at Wembley, Harry Redknapp decided to give Danny Rose his first start for the club and his faith in the youngster paid off.

Danny's goal was also voted the Premier League Goal of the Season by Sky Sports News viewers.

1st

Danny's View

"I was going to bring it down but then at the last minute I thought I'd just hit it, and I caught it so sweetly that it flew in the back of the net.

"My first thought was to just run!

"I ran to look for my Dad and remembered where he was sitting, so I managed to see him. But then the next thing I know I'd turned around and Arsenal were taking the kick-off so I had to run back and defend!"

For the record – That's the second year in a row that a goal against Arsenal has won the Club's Goal of the Season award.

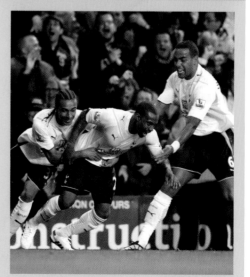

Defoe scores five in incredible win!

Remember the day – November 22nd 2009...

History was made as Jermain Defoe hit five of the goals in our biggest win in over 30 years and put in as good a performance as you will see anywhere - an incredible 9-1 victory over Wigan Athletic at the Lane!

It was the second biggest win in Premier League history. Believe it or not, we were only 1-0 up at half-time! Peter Crouch gave us an early lead but the floodgates opened in the second half.

Defoe took his tally to 12 for the season and looked in unstoppable form as he became only the third player in Premier League history to score five goals in a game. Aaron Lennon, substitute David Bentley, and Niko Kranjcar also got in on the act in a memorable victory.

TOTTENHAM 9
WIGAN 1

Spurs (4-4-2): **Gomes; Corluka, Dawson, Woodgate, Assou-Ekotto (Bassong, 80); Lennon (Bentley, 78), Huddlestone, Palacios (Jenas, 83), Kranjcar; Crouch, Defoe**
Subs not used: **Alnwick, Hutton, Keane, Pavlyuchenko**

Wigan (4-5-1): **Kirkland; Melchiot (Cho, 85), Boyce, Bramble, Edman; N'Zogbia, Diame, Scharner, Thomas (Gomez, 67), Rodallega; Scotland**
Subs not used: **Pollitt, Figueroa, Koumas, Sinclair, Kapo**

BE IN
ONE
GREAT TEAM THIS SEASON

FREE FOR UNDER 11s THIS SEASON

Join One Hotspur for free* and get a goodie bag,
ticket priority and much more.

JOIN ONLINE AT TOTTENHAMHOTSPUR.COM

OR CALL 0844 844 0102

* Lilywhite membership – Free
  Bronze membership – £5

ONE HOTSPUR KICKERS™

TO DARE IS TO DO

Quiz Answers

Who am I?
(From Page 36)

A - DAVID BENTLEY
B - GOMES
C - JERMAIN DEFOE
D - PETER CROUCH

Wordsearch
(From Page 37)

```
C O R L U K A Q H B E H C A B
F U F H R Y P R S D O U M L V
H F G G D T E W E G S D V S X
J F H N I A B C W A B D Y N M
K V J V D K W X M P T L I V G
G L A M J E L S L X M E R H Z
U E O L X I F X O Y D S S A L
F N P H G C A O A N S T D L I
S N F M Q A I Q E N E O M I T
M O D R I C W R A Y D N N W V
D N G C G F N K Z P E E N Z T
C E O K Q E U L B O T A H R I
B D M P B B B B A C R O U C H
O C E H M I N Y L U K M U I I
B Y S T O M N F E J B K I N G
```

Super Spurs Quiz
(From Page 44)
1. 4th
2. Sandro
3. Chelsea
4. Peter Crouch
5. Peter Crouch, Ledley King,
   Michael Dawson, Aaron Lennon
   & Jermain Defoe
6. Five
7. Ossie Ardiles & Ricardo Villa
8. Portsmouth
9. True
10. Gary Mabbutt
11. Honduras
12. Gareth Bale
13. Southampton
14. Luka Modric
15. 24

How did you do?
15
The ultimate Spurs supporter

11-14
Impressive, make sure you get all
15 in the 2012 Annual!

7-10
Mid-table finish

1-6
Do you support Arsenal?

TOTTENHAM HOTSPUR™

Results, Trophies & Stats

Major Honours

Football League Champions **1950-51, 1960-61**

FA Cup Winners **1900-01, 1920-21, 1960-61, 1961-62, 1966-67, 1980-81, 1981-82, 1990-91**

Football League Cup Winners **1970-71, 1972-73, 1998-99, 2007-08**

European Cup-Winners Cup Winners **1962-63**

UEFA Cup Winners **1971-72, 1983-84**

FA Charity Shield Winners **1920-21, 1951-52, 1961-62, 1962-63, 1967-68 (joint), 1981-82 (joint), 1991-92 (joint)**

Results 2009-10

AUGUST 2009

				H	A	
16 Sun	Home	Liverpool	Barclays Premier League	2	1	N/A
19 Wed	Away	Hull City	Barclays Premier League	5	1	24735
23 Sun	Away	West Ham	Barclays Premier League	2	1	33095
26 Wed	Away	Doncaster	Carling Cup	5	1	12923
29 Sat	Home	Birmingham	Barclays Premier League	2	1	35318

SEPTEMBER 2009

				H	A	
12 Sat	Home	Man Utd	Barclays Premier League	1	3	35785
20 Sun	Away	Chelsea	Barclays Premier League	0	3	41623
23 Wed	Away	Preston	Carling Cup	5	1	16533
26 Sat	Home	Burnley	Barclays Premier League	5	0	35462

OCTOBER 2009

				H	A	
03 Sat	Away	Bolton	Barclays Premier League	2	2	21305
17 Sat	Away	Portsmouth	Barclays Premier League	2	1	20821
24 Sat	Home	Stoke City	Barclays Premier League	0	1	36031
27 Tue	Home	Everton	Carling Cup	2	0	35843
31 Sat	Away	Arsenal	Barclays Premier League	0	3	60103

NOVEMBER 2009

				H	A	
07 Sat	Home	Sunderland	Barclays Premier League	2	0	N/A
22 Sun	Home	Wigan Athletic	Barclays Premier League	9	1	35650
28 Sat	Away	Aston Villa	Barclays Premier League	1	1	39866

DECEMBER 2009

				H	A	
01 Tue	Away	Man Utd	Carling Cup	0	2	57212
06 Sun	Away	Everton	Barclays Premier League	2	2	34003
12 Sat	Home	Wolves	Barclays Premier League	0	1	36012
16 Wed	Home	Man City	Barclays Premier League	3	0	35891
19 Sat	Away	Blackburn	Barclays Premier League	2	0	26490
26 Sat	Away	Fulham	Barclays Premier League	0	0	25679
28 Mon	Home	West Ham	Barclays Premier League	2	0	35994

JANUARY 2010

				H	A	
02 Sat	Home	Peterborough	FA Cup	4	0	35862
16 Sat	Home	Hull City	Barclays Premier League	0	0	35729
20 Wed	Away	Liverpool	Barclays Premier League	0	2	42016
23 Sat	Home	Leeds United	FA Cup	2	2	35750
26 Tue	Home	Fulham	Barclays Premier League	2	0	35467
30 Sat	Away	Birmingham	Barclays Premier League	1	1	27238

FEBRUARY 2010

				H	A	
03 Wed	Away	Leeds United	FA Cup	3	1	37704
06 Sat	Home	Aston Villa	Barclays Premier League	0	0	35899
10 Wed	Away	Wolves	Barclays Premier League	0	1	27992
14 Sun	Away	Bolton	FA Cup	1	1	13596
21 Sun	Away	Wigan Athletic	Barclays Premier League	3	0	16165
24 Wed	Home	Bolton	FA Cup	4	0	31436
28 Sun	Home	Everton	Barclays Premier League	2	1	35912

MARCH 2010

				H	A	
06 Sat	Away	Fulham	FA Cup	0	0	24533
13 Sat	Home	Blackburn	Barclays Premier League	3	1	35474
20 Sat	Away	Stoke City	Barclays Premier League	2	1	27545
24 Wed	Home	Fulham	FA Cup	3	1	35432
27 Sat	Home	Portsmouth	Barclays Premier League	2	0	35870

APRIL 2010

				H	A	
03 Sat	Away	Sunderland	Barclays Premier League	1	3	43184
11 Sun	Wembley	Portsmouth	FA Cup	0	2	84602
14 Wed	Home	Arsenal	Barclays Premier League	2	1	36041
17 Sat	Home	Chelsea	Barclays Premier League	2	1	35814
24 Sat	Away	Man Utd	Barclays Premier League	1	3	75268

MAY 2010

				H	A	
01 Sat	Home	Bolton	Barclays Premier League	1	0	35852
05 Wed	Away	Man City	Barclays Premier League	1	0	47370
09 Sun	Away	Burnley	Barclays Premier League	2	4	21161

PLAYER	LEAGUE APPS	LEAGUE GOALS	FA CUP APPS	FA CUP GOALS	LEAGUE CUP APPS	LEAGUE CUP GOALS
B Alnwick	1 (0)	0	0 (0)	0	0 (0)	0
B Assou-Ekotto	29 (1)	1	3 (0)	0	1 (0)	0
G Bale	18 (5)	3	8 (0)	0	3 (0)	0
S Bassong	25 (3)	1	7 (0)	0	3 (0)	0
D Bentley	11 (4)	1	4 (1)	1	4 (0)	1
K Boateng	0 (0)	0	0 (0)	0	0 (1)	0
D Button	0 (0)	0	0 (0)	0	0 (1)	0
V Corluka	29 (0)	1	5 (0)	0	1 (1)	0
P Crouch	21 (17)	8	6 (0)	1	2 (1)	4
C Cudicini	6 (1)	0	0 (0)	0	1 (0)	0
M Dawson	25 (4)	2	8 (0)	0	3 (0)	0
J Defoe	31 (3)	18	6 (1)	5	2 (0)	1
R Fredericks	0 (0)	0	0 (0)	0	0 (0)	0
G Dos Santos	0 (1)	0	0 (0)	0	2 (0)	0
H Gomes	31 (0)	0	8 (0)	0	3 (0)	0
E Gudjohnsen	3 (8)	1	1 (2)	1	0 (0)	0
T Huddlestone	33 (0)	2	5 (1)	0	3 (1)	2
A Hutton	1 (7)	0	2 (0)	0	4 (0)	0
J Jenas	9 (10)	1	2 (0)	0	2 (0)	0
Y Kaboul	8 (2)	0	0 (0)	0	0 (0)	0
R Keane	15 (5)	6	1 (1)	1	2 (1)	2
L King	19 (1)	2	1 (0)	0	0 (0)	0
N Kranjcar	19 (5)	6	5 (3)	2	0 (0)	0
A Lennon	20 (2)	3	0 (0)	0	1 (1)	0
J Livermore	0 (1)	0	0 (0)	0	0 (0)	0
L Modric	21 (4)	3	7 (0)	0	0 (0)	0
K Naughton	0 (1)	0	0 (1)	0	1 (0)	0
J O'Hara	0 (2)	0	0 (0)	0	1 (0)	1
W Palacios	29 (4)	1	6 (1)	0	3 (0)	0
R Pavlyuchenko	8 (8)	5	2 (4)	4	2 (0)	1
D Rose	1 (0)	1	1 (2)	0	0 (1)	0
K Walker	2 (0)	0	0 (0)	0	0 (0)	0
J Woodgate	3 (0)	0	0 (0)	0	0 (0)	0

Where's Chirpy?